For Bertha
love,
Sue

June 2010

Messages from Light

SUZANNE MARGARET SEAMAN

Copyright © 2010, Suzanne Margaret Seaman.
All rights reserved.

Without limiting the rights under copyright reserved above, no part of this publication may be reproduced, stored in or introduced into a retrieval system, or transmitted, in any form or by any means (electronic, mechanical, photocopying, recording or otherwise), without the prior written permission of both the copyright owner and the publisher of this book.

151 Howe Street, Victoria BC Canada V8V 4K5

For information and bulk orders, please contact
info@agiopublishing.com or go to
www.agiopublishing.com

Visit the author's website at
www.SuzanneMSeaman.ca

ISBN 978-1-897435-25-0 (trade paperback)

10 9 8 7 6 5 4 3 2 1 b

Printed on acid-free paper.

This book is dedicated, with gratitude,
to my dear friend Elaine Bugatto, who has shared the journey
of *Messages from Light* with me from the very beginning and
who never stopped believing in the project.

Foreword

" The things that we open ourselves to always come to us. People in olden times expected to see angels and they saw them; but there is no more reason why they should have seen them than that we should see them now; no more reason why they should come and dwell with them than that they should come and dwell with us; for the great laws governing all things are the same today as they were then. If angels come not to minister unto us it is because we do not invite them; it is because we keep the door closed through which they otherwise might enter. "

~ Ralph Waldo Trine

Table of Contents

Introduction   i

Part One
Angels—Who they are and what they do   1

Part Two
Angels—What they say   7
Angelic Consciousness   9
Consciousness   11
Consciousness of Animals   13
Consciousness of Plants   14
Anima   15
Other Life Forms   16
Nature Energy   17
Anatomy   18
How Animals Communicate   19
Interspecies Communication   20
Energy   21
Supernatural   22
Planetary Consciousness   24
Intergalactic Dimensions   25
Intergalactic Communication   27
Intergalactic Co-operation   29
Technology   30
Gravity   32
Evolution of Weather   33
Dimensions   34
Mathematics   35
No Time   36
The Nature of Life Itself   38
How to Manifest   39
Talent   41
Finding Your Lifework   42
Abundance   43
Reality   45
Death   47
Life After Death   49
Reincarnation   51
Ascension   52

Healing	53			
Healing Through God	55			
The Energy of Love	57			
Telepathy	59			
Animal Rights	60			
Food	62			
The Food Chain	64			
Vegetarianism	65			
The New Age	67	Meditation	76
Lightbody	68	Prayer	77
Love	69	Peace on Earth	79
Light	70	Ascended Masters	80
Forgiveness	71	Freedom	81
Happiness	72	Free Will	83
Hope	74	Art	84
		Music	85
		Religion	86
		Thought	87
		Kindness	89
		Gratitude	90
		Humour	91
		Children	93
		The Soul	95
		The God of You	97
		Faith	98

Introduction

I was living in the heart of the magnificent Rocky Mountains of British Columbia when this adventure began. It was 1983. Shortly before, I had moved from Vancouver Island to the Golden area of British Columbia, because I had fallen in love with those mountains, and wanted to live in them. I'd packed all of my worldly goods into my old station wagon; along with my dog Rosie, and didn't stop driving until we got there.

I rented a small log cabin, up on a hill. It had a woodstove for heat, a loft for sleeping, and a kitchen with just enough room for a table to eat at. Outside the front door ran a fast-flowing creek whose ice-cold water tasted sweet, and when you looked up, your eyes feasted upon snow-capped mountains, in every direction. Clearly, I had landed in heaven. Before long, I'd found a job and settled in to the community.

One day, I heard about two well-known psychics in town and I made an appointment to see one of them. In the reading, this woman told me that I would be doing something called automatic writing and she talked about the role that it would play in my life. She explained that this is writing which originates from outside of you, and she then proceeded to instruct me on how to develop it. I went home that day and began to follow her suggestions.

And the automatic writing did begin to flow, just as she said that it would. Over the years, different energies have communicated with me, or have been channeled, using this process. However, the guides who dictated the material in this book originate from the angelic kingdom and are the entities with whom I still enjoy an ongoing connection. We all have angels working alongside of us and who are tirelessly cheering us on. They are amazing beings; messengers of light who uplift, inform and guide us. And now, they will speak for themselves.

~ Suzanne Margaret Seaman

Part One

Angels

Who they are and what they do

When these entities came through and identified themselves as angels, I was surprised to say the very least. I had lots of questions for them; like, what are angels, anyway?

What we are is energy that originates from the sixth dimension. We are beings of light that bring light from our dimension into yours. We are messengers of light and love and we have been given the assignment of connecting all life forms with their own intrinsic divinity.

WHAT ELSE DO THEY DO?

Angels link you to God, or the bigger picture. Angels provide ongoing assistance in each moment of your life. Angels protect you from situations that are not conducive to your higher growth and they propel you towards situations that are. Angels also do their best to bring light to the physical plane ~ they do this in many ways. We do our best to link you with your original purpose for this, your current incarnation. Angels also oversee the birth process as well as the death process, which of course, in reality, is a birth as well.

Angels are everywhere. We work in tandem with nature energy and spirits. We work with people and with animals. We have no form, per se, but we choose appropriate forms for specific assignments. We do our work with love. We do our work *through* love. We do God's work just as you do when you work from your divine centre of light. We are all connected to, and through, light ~ the energy of love. We are all interconnected expressions of consciousness. Each life is an expression of God. This includes each and every life form. Angels are the go-betweens of dimensions; we link each dimension with each other and we bridge them. We bring the vibration of light into where it is needed. We bring hope into where hope is needed. The world has always been hungry for light and hope and reassurance. As angels, we bring the vibrations of these into the world of physical matter. We remind those who are in it, at the time, of their celestial origins. All energy comes from light and returns to light.

We are as close to you as your own self. We are with you in every moment of every day and we love you so much that it may be inconceivable to you. We love you and protect you. We're always with you and we bring light into your heart.

We realize that it is difficult to put faith in what is invisible to the eye, but you are showing great faith by communicating with us. We do assure you that we exist. We exist in a framework of reality not unlike your own. We exist as you yourself do. Fundamentally, we all exist in a place where time and space do not. We simply vibrate at a rate that is quicker than your own.

Thank you for allowing us into your consciousness and into your life.

Thank you for your demonstrations of faith in our kingdom. Thank you for giving us the benefit of the doubt and for allowing us to work alongside of you to bring about a lovely state of awareness into the world. Take heart and let your light shine in a world that is in need of light and love. Have faith in us. Have faith in God and have faith in the God which lives in everything.

We work with you on several levels: the emotional, the mental, the physical and the metaphysical. We are with you also in your dream state. We feel it would be a good idea to spend some time in active meditation with the goal of linking yourself with our kingdom. It is in this way that we will be even better able to help you in the third dimension. We would like to suggest that you begin to strongly sense us. That is to say, visualize us, in angelic form, as we surround you and beam the light of love into your energy field. See us working alongside of you as you move through your day. Feel us as we infuse you with our vibrations. Hear us as we sing you to sleep. Know that you are always safe and that you belong to this world.

AND

Do not worry about your life. Do not worry about the details, but align yourself with God and follow your spirit to wherever it may lead you. Dear heart, be at peace today and every day henceforth. Be at peace and rest in the arms of God who loves you beyond what words can say. You are wondering who or what God is. God is the totality of light, love and consciousness. In other words, God is the big picture. God is not a person. God is awareness. God is the highest vibration of all. God is love. Love is God. Light is God, dark is God and God is everything in between. We are God's emissaries. We bring his energy to Earth. We bring hope and light and love from this vibration to yours.

MOREOVER, THEY SAY THAT

Whoever would like to communicate with their angels is able to. There are as many ways to do it as there are angels and people. We communicate with you through automatic writing because you have experience with it, but we could just as easily communicate with you in other ways. Many people talk with their angels in a religious setting, because they believe that is the only context in which it is possible to do so. Some people only talk to God, or angels, when they find themselves in dire straits. However, one can speak with us at any time, and we welcome all communication and recognition. We exist to be of service to mankind. We are here to bring light and hope to the world, and how much better we are able to do this when you are in conscious communication with our kingdom. Know, then, that all may make contact with their angels, and that we are all waiting for you to do so. For when we link with you, we bring an even higher vibration of light into your being, which then radiates outward to all life that you touch. Imagine, then, how much light could be generated in this world as more and more people open to their angels. What a brightly shining place this would be.

Part Two

Angels

What they say

When you want to
experience something,
simply invite it in and
allow it to show up. It will.

Angelic Consciousness

The consciousness of angels is very different from that of man. It differs in many ways, but the prevailing difference lies in our ability to see through time and space, as well as through dimensions of varying frequencies, or vibrations.

We, in angelic form, do not incarnate in physical form. We do not use physical expression; however, we can appear to take a physical form if it is required. As angels, we are charged with bringing light, love and hope from our kingdom to yours. We perceive energy in terms of light. We are conductors of light. We never give up in our efforts to infuse the consciousness of man with love, light and hope. We never miss an opportunity to connect the soul to the vibrations of these. Often, the soul receives the connection on an unconscious level.

We, in angelic form, are not subject to physical limitations, or laws; therefore our consciousness does not require a physical vehicle. Therefore,

How beautiful a day this is on planet Earth. How beautiful and how perfect. It is difficult to see the perfection of the world from where you sit, but from our perspective, it is a lovely place.

we are neither born nor do we die. This does not mean, however, that we are not growing in every way. We are. We are also involved in ascension and we are always learning. We are always growing and learning, and experiencing this, and other worlds. We are always close to both man and God. We are always washed and renewed in the love of God. It is this love that fuels us, and it is this love that we want to share with you. We are ever with you and we are ever filling your consciousness with the awareness of your own divinity. How dearly we love you, and how dearly we hold you. We do this with all of life and we entreat you to do the same, for we are all sacred, no matter what we do, or do not look like.

Know that it is our great pleasure
to join our energy today
with yours. We honour you.

Consciousness

Consciousness is another word for awareness. To become fully conscious is to become light-filled, and to become light-filled is to become fully aware. The process of attaining God-consciousness is a process of spiritual evolution and this is the path that we are all on. We include ourselves, because angels also evolve. Although we exist outside of the reincarnational spiral, we change and grow in consciousness, too.

Consciousness is multi-faceted. At any one time, a person is able to perceive any amount of information at once. This is because of the nature of the brain's ability to see in a 360-degree circle. However, an individual seldom uses this faculty. Rather, he or she generally uses only a fraction of it. In the dream-state, however, cultural restraints relax, and an individual uses far more of the consciousness that he or she has access to. We would like to say that people on this planet are now opening up in terms of consciousness and that the ramifications of this opening are enormous. With an increase of global consciousness comes enormous spiritual evolution, and with spiritual evolution comes a change to the planet itself. It is a leap forward into light, and beautiful to see. The way that it looks to us, is light that emanates from the planet, rises upward and streams out into the heavens. It is a light of a beautiful luminescent quality, and the colours are all contained in the whiteness of it. This light is the light of heightened awareness and is coming from an increased rate of vibration. As the rate of vibration continues to rise, the Earth herself will increase her speed of movement. She will accelerate and travel more quickly in her orbit. Because all of life is connected, when consciousness is raised in one area, it will help to raise it in others. The best that an individual can do for another is to live in a fully conscious way. We help others by helping ourselves reach a connection to our own divinity ~ the part of us that is God. Once again, we include ourselves here, as well. From where we are, we can see the Earth and the people on her, step into a new frequency of consciousness, and this consciousness is what you call love. The light of it is remarkable and it makes us very happy to see it. We would also like to say that as you step into the light, we are here to help you cross over the threshold into limitlessness. For it is limitlessness that we are all moving toward, and it is limitlessness that we will arrive at.

Practice seeing the God in everything, and in yourself.

Consciousness of Animals

Animals have varying degrees of consciousness. There are species on Mother Earth, which, in terms of consciousness, are in advance of your own. We refer here to the large mammals that live in your oceans. These whales and dolphins have a very large world-view, and they are able to view the developments of the planet from a wide perspective. It is also a compassionate perspective.

The consciousness of all beings is evolving. The time will come when all beings that walk the Earth, swim the oceans and fly the skies, will be in conscious rapport with each other. The time will come when all species will live in harmony with one another. This is what is meant by the lion lying down with the lamb. When consciousness has risen to the level of love, this will manifest as complete interspecies harmony. This evolution of consciousness will take place in the 21st century. It will mark the beginning of a new age of peace and goodwill amongst the inhabitants of Mother Earth. There will be an honouring of one another's vibration and an understanding of one another's needs and desires. There will be a purity of action and beauty of purpose ~ it will truly be heaven on Earth. For what is heaven, but a state of divine consciousness?

Consciousness of Plants

Plants have a different consciousness from that of the animal world, in that they do not have emotions of their own. Rather, they react to the emotions of those who do. They also have a consciousness that extends out past itself. This is true of all plants and trees alike. They have the ability to perceive themselves within a planetary context and indeed, their perspective is a lovely one.

In order to tap into, and experience this consciousness, we suggest that you simply intend to. With the plant or tree that you choose, enter into a state of receptivity. With practice, you will receive impressions from the plant, or tree. You may receive a vibration, a feeling, an idea, or words. When you do this over a period of time, you will develop an understanding of both the process and the consciousness that you are accessing.

Everything in your life, and we do mean everything, is your teacher.

Anima

Anima is the energy that animates all life ~ it is energy that has God at its source. Because all energy, or anima, originates from God, all life is filled with, and supported by, God. God is the energy behind all that is living and all that has ever lived. God is the wind in every sail, and the light in every window. God is the force in every thought, dream and action. God is the shelter in every storm. We would like to say that if you realized that God is in, and outside, of everything, then you would begin to treat yourselves, and everything (as well as everyone) with a sense of reverence, for you would know that you are joined to all life, and the point at which you are joined is at your source. The anima that flows through you is the anima that flows through all of life, in each of its myriad expressions. It is the thread that joins you to each other, and it is the thread that links your consciousness together, and the path along which you may communicate one with another. What makes it possible for you to join your consciousness with another's, is that you both have the same origins and therefore you have the ability to share each other's awareness. This is the reason that you may communicate with any life form you choose. Each one is animated by God and is experiencing God in its own way. We encourage communication between all of God's children.

Other Life Forms

The time is coming shortly on planet Earth when other life forms will be manifesting themselves. The purpose of this is to demonstrate that humans share the cosmos with an enormous variety of fellow beings. These entities, for the most part, are peaceful souls who are on a mission to introduce themselves as representatives of their various cultures. These entities want the inhabitants of this planet to recognize their place within the larger scheme of things ~ they want to point to the bigger picture. When these entities begin to appear, there will be a split consciousness that receives them. Roughly one half of the inhabitants of this plane will be prepared to welcome them, and one half will not. This will begin to occur soon and this is going to be an exciting time in the history of Earth.

You are connected to all of life, and
all of life sings the same song of love.

Nature Energy

There is a range within nature, of energy that spans several dimensions. It moves from the visible through to the invisible. The vibrations form a spectrum that includes a vast network of varying consciousness. Everyone has heard about elves, nature sprites, gnomes, etc. These all exist and more. Mankind has consciously begun to work with nature, and this is true evolution. When different life forms begin to work in conscious harmony, then the planet has begun to heal itself. In this world, there is a purpose for each energy. There is a plan for each life. Remember that all life is moving toward completion of itself. All life is moving upward into light and totality of consciousness. All life is interconnected, and all life is sacred. We would suggest that humans recognize their place within the spectrum of nature energy. We suggest that although consciousness varies between all life, no one life is inherently more valuable than another. Once mankind begins to view other life energy from a wider perspective, he will begin to see the truth of this for himself. We are also a part of the spectrum, and we work closely with others that are not visible to the human eye.

Anatomy

Anatomy is often thought of as being synonymous with destiny. This is not always the case, however. Know that the physical form that you now use is temporary, indeed. Know that in your physical incarnations you will express yourself in many types of bodies and you will learn from all of them. You will experience different aspects of your soul in each expression of anatomy. Know that each of your fellow beings is doing the same thing. Therefore, each life is sacred. Each living thing is only temporarily using the physical form in order to gain further life experience.

Know that there is nothing outside of yourself more powerful than what is inside of yourself. What does this mean? It means that you yourself can achieve anything that you want or need. It means that, in truth, no one has real power over you unless you believe that they do. It means that you are a sovereign being in all that you think and do. It means that you are capable of limitless success and triumphs. It means that nothing can truly subjugate you without your express permission. We would suggest that you begin to tap into the reservoir of your own power. You will then experience the God of you.

How Animals Communicate

Animals communicate telepathically. That is, they communicate in visual patterns. They communicate with images that arise from their emotional centres. In other words, they interact with each other from an emotional direction, and the image, or picture, is a projection of it. The image is understood by all and it represents the animal's feelings at the moment. The image also represents the animal's thoughts and desires.

Animals don't think abstractly; they don't think about the future in terms of various possibilities. They live in the present moment ~ they don't project themselves forward into time. They don't worry about the future and they don't hold on to the past. This doesn't mean that they don't have memories; they do. Many have excellent memories. It's just that they don't live in these memories the way that people often do. Also, if animals were able to speak, they would speak from the perspective of now, as opposed to before, or after.

We would like to say that animals do indeed try to send images to people all the time. Some people get them and some do not. When people do receive them, it is done subconsciously. They receive the message telepathically, and then act upon it.

Interspecies Communication

Communication between species is the natural state of things ~ it is the lack of communication which is unnatural. It is unnatural because all life is interconnected and energy runs between all that lives. Because this current of energy flows through the consciousness of all beings; it follows then, that all beings are linked to light and love, and therefore they are linked to each other. In order for Mother Earth to heal herself, all of her children must once again learn to speak the same language. This is the language of love, and it is a language that has no words. This is a language that all beings know and the time is coming when it will be spoken between all who walk, swim and fly. This consciousness will manifest when the changes to this planet bring all beings into a new shared reality. When all beings consciously unite, the light will shine brightly indeed from Mother Earth.

How large is the heart of a dog? Dear hearts, if you could see how brightly the light shines from a happy dog, you would be astounded.

Energy

Energy all comes from one source ~ it comes from God. It comes from the totality of light and love and consciousness. Energy follows its own patterns according to the form it holds. In other words, energy moves along pathways of light that are part of consciousness. Energy changes form when the pathways change direction. This is why nothing ever dies, it only transforms itself. In the not so distant future, mankind will learn how to use energy that is found in nature that does not need to change form in order to be used for various applications. Technology need not rob Mother Earth of her resources. Mankind may use alternative sources of fuels. Mankind need only use what is freely given to him. These gifts will always be given and it is only natural to accept what is given. For God gives with love to his children, and abundance is the natural state of the universe ~ it is a God-given birthright to all who have life. Let's thank God for his blessings and honour his gifts by acknowledging them.

Supernatural

Supernatural phenomena are generally considered to be phenomena for which there is no logical explanation. We would suggest, however, that all phenomena have a natural explanation and all phenomena adhere to natural laws.

There are a great deal of things that mankind is capable of, if only he knew what they are, and how to do them. For example, man is able to travel at the speed of thought, not only with his consciousness, but with his physical body as well. There are people alive today who do. Man is also able to be in more than one place at any one time. You have the ability to divide yourself into two spheres of consciousness for as long as you want or need. You have the ability to go backward or forward through time – you have this freedom available to you. You also have the ability to share consciousness with every life form known to you, as well as with a host of life forms that you have yet to encounter. You also have the ability to see into every dimension that has ever existed and you have the ability to contact all of your selves that exist now on every plane of existence. You have the ability to recognize each other, communicate with each other and to join forces with each other. You have the ability to blend with your soul, and when you become blended with it, to then fully incorporate all of your other selves together into one strong force. This force is a strong light that acts as a beacon to other complete souls. These souls join their energy fields together and serve as clusters of light that show the way for others to follow. You are able to experience heaven here on Earth and transcend form and limitation of every kind. And we, in angelic form, are here to remind you of this.

> Know that everything in this beautiful plane of light is here for a reason. Everything has a purpose and everything is beautiful to he or she who has eyes to see it.

Planetary Consciousness

Planetary consciousness means this: that each planet has its own state of awareness, or consciousness, and there is life of some sort upon each one. Between incarnations, humans often visit various planets for the purpose of benefiting from these various states of consciousness. Certain planets are helpful for learning love, for example. Venus is one of these. Other planets are useful for cultivating the consciousness of world peace and respect for all life. Still others are valuable for the nurturing of personal power.

In order to make the best possible use of these experiences, the soul incorporates them into itself for future reference. This would be comparable to the circuitry of, for example, a computer. The soul uses this information that it has gathered when it makes incarnation decisions. It chooses incarnation situations that will make the best use of its off-planet experiences. These off-planet experiences accumulate and provide rich sources of knowledge. By the time it has stored up many such experiences, we call this an old soul. When an old soul has reached the stage of release from the reincarnation spiral, it will be free to stay in the realm of off-planet consciousness. It may then choose from a great variety of vibrations with which to merge.

Intergalactic Dimensions

We would like to say, first of all, that there are almost an unlimited number of galaxies and an almost unlimited variety of expressions of consciousness within them. There are dimensions which contain physical life expression, and dimensions which do not. For example, between incarnations, you often go, in consciousness, to specific dimensions for specific reasons. Sometimes you do this in much the same way that you would make a lunch date with a friend: 'I will meet you right after this lifetime, in the vibration of X, Y, or Z ~ look for me there'. This is something to look forward to. You do not, generally speaking, remember this on a conscious level, but you do on an unconscious level, and when the time comes, you simply go. There are some dimensions that you access from your dream state. When you do, you often bring back exciting revelations with you and these revelations provide you with new insights, hope and direction. We, in angelic form, often work with you from this state. We would also like to say that as the consciousness of

Your desire for truth is a noble one, for in truth lies freedom and in freedom lies acceleration.

man expands, so too does his ability to tap into the full quantity of dimensions that are both all around him and within him. As his consciousness expands, so too will the illusion of separateness that man often feels, dissolve. Man will no longer feel separate from the rest of the cosmos when he finds his own place within it, and when he lets the light of God shine through him. This time is almost at hand.

Dear hearts ~ know that all you perceive with your senses, is illusion. This is the nature of the third dimensional experience. As you transit from the third dimension into the higher dimensions, illusion is replaced with truth and clarity. You can, however, access truth within the third dimension and the way that you do this, is by learning to see and feel with your heart. By taking actions based upon what your heart tells you, you re-align yourself with the power of your soul's purpose and you set yourself free.

Intergalactic Communication

Between all galaxies, there exists a network of communication that is composed of a system of thought and light. This system has always been in place and the way that it functions is this ~ galaxies have unique qualities and vibrations. There is an energy pattern that reflects these qualities and vibrations, much like the aura of an individual life form. Now when the aura of each galaxy reaches out and merges with that of another, they are then in a position to connect and communicate.

How does this affect individuals on each planet within each galaxy? As each individual raises his or her vibratory level, he or she is able to sense not only different states of consciousness, but different systems of consciousness. What we mean is that, as an individual begins to explore alternatives in awareness within his or her self, he or she is, in fact, experiencing communication with other awareness in the cosmos. The advantage of this is that the more we are cognizant of other frequencies of light and thought, the more we are able to link with the totality of consciousness, or God. The more that we are able to link with God, the quicker we are able to merge with him. When we call God 'him', we do so not because God is a person, but because God has been traditionally viewed as one.

God is larger than this, and we could just as easily call God 'she'. We do not mean to give God a gender any more than we could give light, love, or consciousness one.

When individuals on each plane of light begin to sense one another, and feel into what it means to be a part of a larger whole, there will be a spiritual growth amongst all life. As we move toward conscious intergalactic communication, we move toward freedom, for in awareness there is opening, and with opening there is light. In order to step up the process, one can intend that this come about. One can intend to open to all life in all places and in all forms. One can intend to be in conscious communication with the full circle of light, and bring it into oneself ~ this will cause the self to expand into its true cellular blueprint. This will bring about a fullness of consciousness and a unity with self. Intergalactic communication is a physical phenomenon that has ramifications for the individual. It has a positive potential for spiritual expansion.

As above, so below.

Invite your guides, in whatever form they take, into a closer relationship with yourself.

Intergalactic Co-operation

As a species, man is learning that he is not the only life form on his planet with intelligence and that his planet is not the only one that has consciousness. He is learning that there are other planets, as well as other galaxies that support advanced consciousness, and therefore, civilizations of one type or another. The time has come on Earth when man will shortly be able to not only communicate with other such life, but to work together with it, in order to understand the true nature of God who has created life in all of its myriad expressions. Intergalactic co-operation will be commensurate with an expanded consciousness which will manifest in Earth time before long. Indeed, there are many benefits of such an expanded consciousness. We would suggest that people keep their minds open to changes that are happening of a spiritual and metaphysical nature. These are indications of the evolution of consciousness, or ascension.

Technology

Technology is a wonderful thing in itself and we feel that it has vast potential for creating positive events in the world. There are some civilizations throughout your galaxy that have, by your standards, astounding technology. It is technology that is based upon light. Simply put, it uses light and sound, which exist naturally in the universe. These are resources that will not become depleted. This technology converts light and sound into energy that fuels everything from spacecraft to food.

On this planet, technology is also able to do amazing things, but we feel that problems have arisen around it because technology has not grown at the same rate as consciousness has. It has grown faster and this has created an imbalance. This imbalance is evidenced by, for example, war technology. Your leaders have the ability to kill many people at once, but not the love in their hearts to guide them to understand one another. Our message to them is this ~ take the love that you feel for your family and let it fill your heart. Let your heart expand and bring more people in. Learn that all of life is connected and that you cannot cause death to others without bringing it to yourself. If it does not come to your physical self, it will come to your soul. For all of life is precious and all of life is sacred.

We say this ~ do not bring destruction about in the name of God. Do not claim to have God in your corner, for God is life without end, and God is who you are destroying. We would suggest that technology needs to go hand in hand with compassion and spirituality. We would suggest that technology be used to bring about positive results, not negative ones. We would suggest that mankind focus upon its connections, rather than its differences and that technology be a reflection of an expanded consciousness. We would also like to say that we feel technology in itself is not a bad thing; it is the potential that it has for harm that concerns us.

Know that you are capable of bending both time and space in order to enter states of consciousness which you would like to experience. As Earth herself moves into the next level of vibration, you may move with her, simply by knowing that you can. Know that there are portals within the Earth's poles. Perhaps you have read about life beneath the surface of your planet. This exists in an interdimensional framework and has since the beginning of time. You may go there and explore what life looks like there. You do it by understanding that you can straddle several dimensions simultaneously. You can have a foot in each place and remain safe and grounded. You can visit as often as you like and you can bring back your experiences on the conscious level. Dear hearts ~ your world is vaster than you know, and it awaits you.

Gravity

Gravity is a law that operates on this planet and all planets that contain three dimensional life expression. In atmospheres of other dimensions, gravity is not needed.

The time is coming shortly upon Mother Earth when gravity will be used as a means of propulsion. The way that this will work is that the force will be harnessed in such a way as to power engines that draw their primary fuel from other sources. Gravity, in other words, will sustain the momentum of the charge.

Gravity can be used for any number of applications. It will be used for technology in place of electricity. It will be used for transportation that has not yet been developed. It will be used to harness light in order to prolong the growing season of plants and vegetables. It will be used to filter out toxins from your environment, and it will be used in new technologies to clean up the pollution from your water systems. Gravity will prove to be one of the most astounding resources at your disposal.

Know that before long, you will be interacting with technology that will heal you on every level of your being.

Evolution of Weather

Your atmosphere on Earth is an ever-changing thing. Weather today is not the same as it was ten, twenty or thirty years ago; it changes and evolves just as everything does. Outer weather is a direct reflection of inner weather. That is to say, that as consciousness amongst all life evolves, so too does the consciousness of your atmosphere. Weather also reflects the shifts in consciousness as they take place within man. As your planet moves into the new age, weather conditions move along with it. The present turbulence of your weather patterns will increase in intensity for the next few years. This parallels the corresponding turbulence within the psyche of man at this time. Soon, a peace will descend upon Mother Earth, and the very weather itself will be harmonious. The weather will become tranquil all over the globe, and every day will be a lovely day outside. This does not mean that you will no longer experience distinct seasons, you will. For each season outside corresponds to a season within the heart of man, and each season is beautiful in itself. Know then, that the weather does change over time. It keeps pace with the change all around it and it reflects inner evolution.

Dimensions

Each dimension is a different level of existence. You exist on each level at any one time, and yet your consciousness will primarily be focussed upon the third dimension. This is the dimension of physical reality. The fourth dimension is largely the dimension of thought. It precedes the third, which is manifested thought. The fifth dimension is the dimension of pure energy and light. The sixth dimension is the realm of non-human energy. It is the dimension from which we exist, those of us in angelic form. The seventh dimension is the state of God consciousness. It is the ultimate level of consciousness ~ all that exists here is love. It is difficult from the third dimension perspective to conceive of such a place. Nonetheless, it is there and it is most wonderful. There are no levels past this one, because there is no vibration that is higher than love ~ it is the most powerful vibration of all. May we say that we have been privileged to have a glimpse of this dimension.

Mathematics

Mathematics is a language of the third dimension that leads out into the fourth. What we mean here, is that mathematics is the language that describes the physical form of the third dimension, and higher mathematics describes the fourth dimension. It is a connection that is not well understood.

Branches of mathematics that deal with integers and decimals are branches of mathematics rooted in the physical world. Branches of mathematics that deal with physics actually relate to the world of metaphysics. If one were to study physics with a view to this cosmic connection, one could access the world in a fresh new way. One could discover, for example, the origins of all language. One could trace the evolution of the physical world. One could gain an understanding of the concept of limitlessness, which we realize is a difficult image to grasp.

Mathematics is an entry point into infinity and a tool that you can use to access it. The time will come when you will simply bypass all language, including mathematics, and arrive at any destination you can conceive of. This will happen as consciousness on a global scale moves into, and operates from, the fourth dimension.

No Time

Truly, time does not exist. It never has. Time is a unit of measurement that has been devised by man in order to provide him with a chronological framework. Man found this framework necessary in order to make sense of his experiences. Neurologically, man finds it difficult to imagine that everything inside and outside himself is happening simultaneously. In point of fact, however, it is. Other species on this planet do not keep track of time. They are scarcely aware of such a concept. The measurements that they use are biological, and this is all that they need.

Because there is no such thing as time, the past, present and future are illusions. What does this mean? It means that all of your lives, both on and off planet, are happening simultaneously and they are happening now. How is this possible? It is possible because you are, generally speaking, focussing on only one life expression at a time. If you were to choose to experience

> The best time to be in is the present moment, for it is within the present moment that your power lies. Let it flow through you and all other moments will take care of themselves.

your other selves, you could. You would do this through meditation or dreams.

Because you are living all of your lives at once, this does not invalidate reincarnation. This is because you have believed in time throughout all of your past lifetimes. This has given you a sense of chronology and terms of reference. What it does mean, however, is that you have total access to these lives both past and future. This is because you are experiencing them concurrently with this one. Access them by knowing that you can.

What this also means is that you can heal yourself of all imbalances on every level by becoming aware of their origins. In other words, when you are able to take a close look at some or all of your other selves, you are then in a position to identify the sources of some of your imbalances.

Do this by knowing that you can. Do this to discover where you developed certain belief structures that may be causing you ill health or lack on some other level.

Know then, that time does not exist but was invented to give form and structure to man's experiences on Earth. Know that, because it is an artificial construct, you can move freely within it, whenever you choose. This is a freedom that you can use for your growth. This is an expression of limitlessness that we are all a part of.

The Nature of Life Itself

Life was never intended to be a struggle, nor was it intended to become very complicated. Life on Earth is intended by God to be a joyous affair. It is intended to be fun, for indeed one can learn and progress at the same time as being happy and feeling light and free. This, in our opinion, is the best way to feel. As we, in angelic form, watch mankind go about his daily life, we so want him to look up and take refreshment from the sky. We want him to feel the light that we infuse into his energy field, and into his very soul. We want him to focus on light and on love and feel joy in his heart. How dear he is to us. We feel it would be a good idea to remember that life is a journey that we all embark upon quite willingly. Let's not forget that we are all here by choice and that we are here to learn, amongst other things, that we are to be happy in ourselves. All is growth and ascension and light. Let's be kind to one another. Let's be gentle and see God in everything.

> *Your own heart is your road map home. When you follow your heart, you link yourself to the heart of God. When you are linked to God, then you can allow God's energies to work through you.*

How to Manifest

Free will is a gift that enables you to find your way into a state of limitlessness. In other words, if you as a species did not have it, you would surrender your control over your own self and over your own destinies. Therefore, you have the ability to transcend the physical through use of the will, and thereby alter the physical. This is possible for everyone on Earth at this time.

Intentions form the basis of your life experiences. You create a picture of what you want in your mind's eye, and then you fully intend to have it. You join your will to your heart's desires and bring them into being in the third dimension. Expect your heart's desires to come, as this pulls them in from our dimension into yours. Your expectations magnetize them into physical reality. This is the law of manifestation: you intend that something will manifest, and then you expect it. You increase the speed of its arrival by visualizing the manifested thing or state. When the manifestation arrives, then you thank yourself for creating it, and then you create something else. The time will come when people will be able to manifest what they want instantaneously ~ this is a few generations away and will come as a result of an increased rate of vibration.

> Your mission is as unique as yourself and know that only you can identify it.

Now, in order to manifest your heart's desires, you need to feel strongly about them. The stronger you desire something; the stronger will be your ability to bring it in to the physical dimension. When you have visualized fully what it is that you want, and have visualized yourself with it, strongly feel the joy that it brings you. Be sure to feel it as thoroughly as possible. See and hear yourself telling others about it, and see them sharing their joy with you. When you do, visualize them also manifesting their hearts' delights. In this way, the energy of abundance becomes magnified and brought up to a conscious level.

Know that you can have anything that you can conceive of. Know that one of the lessons of the third dimension that you are all here to learn is the art of manifestation and it is not a difficult law to master. It is part of the process of coming into your own power, or divinity. Manifestation is what you do every day. We would suggest that you remove all limitations from what you presently believe you are able to create. You can create anything. Therefore, we say search your heart and discover what it is that you want to experience at this time. Believe that you can create it, give thanks for it, and allow it to manifest.

Talent

Everyone has at least one talent and some people have many. The purpose of having a talent is that every talent fills a need that the universe has ~ in other words; each talent is needed in the world. Therefore, each talent needs to be expressed, and ideally used for the highest good of all. When one begins to use one's talents in this way, one's life begins to work on all levels. If a person is blessed with many talents, let him or her develop the talent that draws him or her the most. Always do what makes you feel alive and happy. In this way, life becomes a journey of growth and joy. It also becomes a state of abundance.

Know that as you work with the principle of intent, you will bring into manifestation everything that you seek. You can intend anything into being that you want to. If you seek answers, intend that you will receive them by a certain 'time' and intend to have the universe bring them to you. Remember to keep your heart open so that God can shine through it. Be the window that the sun shines through.

Finding Your Lifework

*I*n order to find your lifework, you need not look very far ~ it will always be associated with something that you really love, or love to do. Generally speaking, this is something that you have loved from an early age and that you gravitate towards. It is something that inspires you, fascinates you, and energizes you. We would suggest that when a person identifies what this is, the next step involves finding a way to turn this love into a service. In other words, how can you take this activity, or thing that you love, and while interacting with it, help other people in the process? How can you take it and help the world? How can you do it and raise consciousness as you go?

We would suggest that you begin to desire the highest quality of life possible for yourself. This intention will create the road that it will travel upon to meet you.

When you have found answers to these questions, you have discovered your lifework. This is almost always what you came in to do in this incarnation. It may be an interest that you have explored in other lifetimes. In any case, when you discover what it is, and begin it, this is when your life truly begins. This is when you align your energy with the energy of the cosmos itself.

Abundance

Abundance is truly the natural state of the universe ~ it is a God-given state of plenty that exists for all beings. When abundance doesn't seem present, it is a matter of perception. Financial abundance is the result of several things. It is a result of a belief that one is worthy of enjoying financial abundance, and it is also a result of believing that financial abundance is the natural state of affairs in this world. It also comes from having all of one's energy open and flowing ~ by having one's psychic, emotional and physical energy circulating and moving within and outside of one's self.

One can tap into financial abundance in a number of ways. One can do whatever it is one loves to do: this will bring financial prosperity. One can also intend to have it and by this we mean that one can will it in. We

> *You are here on Earth to do what it is you love. We are all here to do this ~ we who have never incarnated, and you who have. We are here to love, and be loved, and to share love with all of life. We are here to taste life and to drink it deeply. We are here to experience.*

would suggest that if one does this, then one also say: "for the highest good of all." In this way, personal will is linked with divine will and this will improve the results. One can also bring in financial abundance through all the regular channels. We would suggest, however, that one bear in mind the spiritual laws of money, and they are these: that money is simply a symbol of energy ~ in itself it is nothing. Money represents an energy exchange and this exchange is an important one in the third dimension. A lack of money is not a noble thing ~ there is no inherent spiritual value in poverty. Money, once it is brought in, increases in value as it is shared with others. As one shares energy with others, it increases also in quantity. And, that money itself does not make people act in negative ways ~ it is what is inside the individual that determines the way that they handle the money, or the lack of it. Financial abundance is your birthright. Let it in and enjoy it. As we have said previously, life was never meant to be a struggle.

Reality

Reality is not a thing that can be measured, or compared, or imposed upon one. Reality is as different as the multiple life forms that have conscious expression. Each being experiences a different one. Each being creates its own reality.

Know that you can create any reality you like. If you want a reality that features a high quality of life, then you can have it. Whatever you are able to conceive, you are able to create and you are able to do this because of your free will.

Choose the reality that you want to experience. Know that you can have it. Begin to visualize yourself enjoying this reality. Begin to feel how this reality feels, and if this reality brings you joy, begin to hold the vibration of joy within you, so that you grow accustomed to it. In this way, you learn to experience the emotional counterpart of the physical reality that you are preparing to have. Continue to see yourself in this new reality, and

Know this ~ that anything you choose to have in this life, is yours. It's true. Choose health. Choose wealth. Choose freedom from all limitations.

feel the way it feels. This will begin to draw toward you the situation that you have created. We would suggest that you continue doing this until the time comes when you feel a shift of consciousness begin to happen. The way it will feel is as if something is now beginning to move toward you. This indicates that you have brought the tools to create your ideal reality into your energy field. Do not, we would suggest, try to imagine what these tools might be. Rather, let the universe bring them to you, knowing that it is especially qualified to do this. The universe is part of the Big Picture, and is able to deliver what you may not be able to imagine. Therefore, it may exceed your fondest dreams. Know that you may have anything you want. Create the reality of it by seeing yourself in it and feeling what it is like. Draw it toward you by putting energy into it, and then, when you have created it, enjoy it.

Everything comes in its own time. Everything has its own rhythm. And everything comes to she who asks.

Death

Death, in your culture, is treated in a fearful way. It is generally not talked about and it is considered something to be avoided as much as possible. However, it is a very sacred and beautiful thing. Death of the physical body is a birth of the spiritual. In other words, death is a glorious transition into a larger consciousness ~ it is a release from physical limitations. The soul is then in a position to determine whether or not to continue with physical expression, or to grow in another direction. People wonder if they will be reunited with loved ones, as they hear about from many sources. The answer is yes. This is beautiful for us to see, beautiful in every way. If people could see how lovely death is, we believe they would not fear it. It is merely a door through which one walks. One of us accompanies each soul in transition, just as we accompany each soul into the world of matter. We do this in life after life. One soul will often work with the same group of angels in all of its successive lives.

Know that death is simply one more step in the ongoing journey into light. It is not something to fear ~ it is about freedom and evolution and light. Death is a process of leaving behind one experience in exchange for another, and for most people, it is a beautiful time. And know that the barrier between the living and the dead is illusory ~ it does not exist.

Be at peace in your transitions. Be at peace in your hearts. Know that everything happens by great design ~ all is as it must be. Have no fear for tomorrow, but let each day take care of itself. It will. And know, dear hearts, that the kingdom of God awaits you all, and the light of it heals all things. God is within you and manifesting through you at every moment. Know that the limits you embrace here do not restrict you as you walk through this door ~ the process of dying is the process of beginning to live fully. For without the body, one is able to expand at an outstanding rate of growth.

Do not be afraid to release yourself from the chains of this world. We are with you, and we bring the vibrations of light and love and peace into your heart. We hold you in love and we carry you forward to your place of rest. For you will rest, dear heart, and you will heal, and you will go onward upon your own path of light.

Life After Death

There is life after death, just as there is life before birth. Indeed, there is always life. Life changes continuously in its expression of self. Just as there is life in the egg before and after it hatches, so there is life in every living thing during all of its life stages. Indeed, there is no such thing as death. Death is an illusion. When the soul leaves its physical body behind, it is free to experience other things. It rejoices in its freedom. The soul has a vast array of choices to choose from for its subsequent development. It may choose, for example, to rest awhile before entering in to another vehicle. It may choose to eliminate the physical expression altogether. It may decide to return to the physical plane in a different form. The object of life is to experience it widely, and this is a good way to do that.

When a soul chooses to continue on the physical expression, it will, for the most part, do so with the companionship of the same group of angels each time. This is done with mutual agreement. In any case, the soul is always in possession of free will to decide everything concerning itself. Free will exists both in and out of body. If the soul chooses to explore other opportunities for growth, there are, again, an almost infinite number of options available to do this. There is no end to the growth that is possible on the path of light. The more distance one travels down it, the brighter one's light becomes. The brighter one's light becomes, the closer one is to home. For home is the heart of God ~ we all come from it and we all return to it.

From our perspective, the cosmos is infinitely vast. You have all had glimpses of it from time to time. You have all had opportunities of floating free within All That Is. Know that you would benefit from remembering these experiences because it would place you within the larger context of who you are. You are not someone who is simply having a series of lifetimes upon planet Earth ~ you are cosmic beings who create experiences in all corners of the omniverse. You are free agents ~ creating, planning and carrying out marvelous intergalactic assignments and adventures. You are infinite.

Reincarnation

Reincarnation is a fact of life. Everyone in human form is in the reincarnation spiral ~ this is the most natural way to widen the experience of life. We want to experience as much as possible, therefore we put ourselves in positions to be able to do so. We say we because even though we, as angels, are outside of the reincarnation spiral, we too are constantly learning and growing.

You have read about the transmigration of souls ~ this involves a change of life form. Whatever form the soul decides to use for its expansion of consciousness, the goal is the same, and that is ultimate blending with God, or light. We have already mentioned that the soul is generally accompanied by the same group of angel companions. This facilitates the process and it aids in the rate of growth that the soul is able to accomplish, particularly between incarnations. This is the time when the soul considers its progress and makes choices for the balance of the journey into light. The soul may choose between male and female, race, geography, family, intellectual ability, and so on. Karmic factors also play a role. When a soul comes to the end of its incarnation cycle, it is free to enjoy consciousness without a physical body ~ this is an exciting development that comes to all, in time.

Ascension

Ascension is evolution, and the prime movement and direction of the universe. That is to say, that evolution of life and consciousness is the rule. Everything is progress, despite appearances. Everything is growth, and everything is spiraling upward into light. This means that all life is in the process of refining itself and increasing its rate of vibration, or consciousness. This is the nature of life ~ to evolve and grow.

Know that the things that you want in your life, also want you. In the same way that you want to experience them, so too do they want to experience you. Remember that everything has consciousness, even that which you consider 'things.' Know that you are always drawing toward you that which you choose to think about. Dear hearts, choose your thoughts with care and consciousness and enjoy this world.

Healing

All healing is done by alignment with one's soul to the soul of God. If you have faith in your ability to create this, or faith in someone else's ability to do this, your healing is available. We cannot do this for you ~ how we wish that we had such power. The truth is, dear hearts, it is you that have this power, and it is you who have forgotten this. We in these forms can only remind you of your own divinity and power. We can only remind you to open the door that you have forgotten was closed.

When the soul is out of alignment with itself, it can attract disease into the body, mind or spirit. Disease becomes manifested when the organism cannot assimilate this new vibration. Many diseases originate from the mind, which is easily influenced by negativity. Some disease comes from past karma and some originates from habits of self-destruction. All healing comes when the soul is able to reconnect itself with light. When one needs healing, one needs to consciously choose to abandon ill health. One needs to intend to be well and one needs to be prepared to let it in. One can heal oneself permanently when one makes the commitment. The commitment sets the forces into action that determine the outcome. Everyone has this ability to bring themselves back into light and health and freedom from illness of any kind. Free will guarantees this. We encourage everyone to become committed to health and abundance on every level.

The most significant things in this world are invisible to the human eye. You cannot see the energy of things. You cannot see, for example, the light of one another, or the ties that connect you. You cannot see the ways in which you are held down by energies that you do not understand. You cannot see, as we do, how humanity fits into the big picture and yet each one of you possesses the ability to do so. Within your DNA lies the dormant abilities that you have had access to before and that you will access once again. Within your DNA lies divinity, your connection to Source. Within your DNA lies your power to evolve into what is coded there and beyond. For your potential, dear hearts, is unlimited and as you move forward, you will easily see, on all levels, that which is invisible to you now.

Healing Through God

We have talked about the nature of healing and now we would like to speak about how you may heal yourself, and others, by channeling the imprint of divine health. The way that this works is this ~ within each being there is a cellular blueprint for total physical, spiritual and emotional health. As beings go through physical expression, they become subjected to, and subject themselves to, many experiences that remove them from this pattern of perfection. Much of this is of a mental and emotional nature. It is possible to bring the being back into alignment with their own blueprint, or imprint. We say being because this applies to all life. The way to do this re-alignment is to stand next to the one in need of healing. Place your hands on their physical body. Surround yourself with light, and see and feel yourself bringing light from God down into your hands. Sense the energy running through the body. What it is doing is restoring the body to its original condition of health. You are doing this by replacing the energy lost due to stress, injury or disease. If the healing is not immediate, it will begin at this time, and continue at a pace that is determined by the being itself. In other words, if someone does not believe that healing can be instantaneous, then this will slow down the procedure.

A person may heal him or herself in this way. Simply draw the energy of God into yourself and feel the light of it flood into you. You will know when to stop. We would like to say that health is a God given right, and therefore it is genetically programmed into your very cells. Re-awaken to this freedom. Claim it. Heal yourself and heal others, and link the God within you to the God outside you. Enjoy total health. Enjoy this life you have chosen.

Most people are familiar with the energy centers known as chakras. These exist within the etheric body and they are the points at which cosmic energy enters the body and regulates it. When a being is fully balanced and in harmony, their chakras are spinning freely and the body is healthy. When the chakras become diminished in size, or enlarged, imbalances turn up in the physical body. Know that one way of keeping the body in physical attunement, is to become aware of one's energy field and the state of one's chakras. You can see them in your mind's eye, through intention, and make adjustments to them as necessary. You can program them to regulate themselves when they are not operating smoothly. Know that there are many more chakras than those which are commonly referred to. You need not know their respective locations in order to bring them into alignment. Simply state your intention that this be done and enjoy the benefits to your being that this adjustment brings.

The Energy of Love

We would suggest that love is the highest vibration there is and that everything in your world and in your experience, is an expression of love. We would also suggest that love is present in all cells of all living things. What you may not know, is that love exists in that which is also not living. What this means is that you can create a love connection with all that is. When you come from your heart, you can not only move mountains, but you can move buildings, too. With an open heart, you can pour love into any object and interact with it on this level. This means that you may bring about change not only in your relationship with an object, but with the object itself. We would suggest that this is because one need not be animated in order to receive love. Know that your appliances, your vehicles, your lamps and your chair not only recognize and receive love, but they are capable of sending love. Therefore, know that the power of love is such that, with it, all things are possible. Know also, that with love, all things are vital. Knowing this, direct love into that which does not seem to work. Direct love into that which does work, and see it work better than it is 'supposed' to. For dear hearts, love is light and light is who you are. There is darkness in light, there is light in darkness and there is

God in everything. See the God in everything and in yourselves. When you do, you will see the perfection, also. It is difficult, where you are, to see the perfection of God in all things, however, you will come to see it.

Dear hearts ~ know that as you move within your spiral of acceleration, you will not only learn to see the God in all things, you will learn to see the joy in all things. You will see into things and situations and find the joy within them. You will come to operate from the light of your own soul, which is a generator of joy and love. For on the soul level, you are always in the present moment, and you are always joyful. Know that you need only focus upon the present moment with an open heart. This is all anyone need do. This is what God does. This is what the masters do and this is what you can do, also.

All kingdoms of life together form God and when all kingdoms are able to share consciousness, this planet will radiate one of the brightest lights in the cosmos. This will come to pass.

Telepathy

Telepathy is the universal system of communication ~ it is the way that all beings communicate with one another. Generally speaking, this takes place on an unconscious level. When you, in human form, choose to communicate with your brothers and sisters in non-human form, the way you do this will be done telepathically. That is to say, that the language you will use will have no words. After you receive the message, your brain will provide words for the transmission.

Telepathy can take several forms. It might take the form of images, or mental pictures, or the telepathy may come in on the vibrations of thought. That is to say, that you will receive the thought form. Or, the telepathy may be emotional.

Telepathy may be practiced, and practice will bring about an effortless two-way communication. The goal is to bring it up to a conscious level. We do encourage telepathic communication because all of life is interconnected, and all of life is ready to be joined together once again as God. This comes from understanding one another, and understanding one another comes from communication.

Animal Rights

The time is coming to Mother Earth when the consciousness of every living being will be recognized. When this happens, all of life will be respected and honoured. Animal rights will be granted. This represents a great leap forward in consciousness and this evolution of consciousness will reflect in a higher quality of life for all.

Know that life on Earth has never been more exciting than now, and you came for the good seats.

When species begin to understand each other better, as a result of inter-species communication, everyone benefits. When animals are accorded their God-given rights, they will then become able to proceed with furthering the goals that they individually and collectively have. Animals do have goals ~ they may be simple or they may be complex. Animals also have free will. Generally speaking, this is often overridden by the free will of another. When animals regain their rights, which have eroded over time, they will be significantly happier in themselves. This is true of all animals alive now that are treated with respect and love. These animals already have equality in the world. We would also like to say that we feel that the time is at hand when all of God's children, in whatever form they live, will know themselves to be equals in every way.

No one life form is more precious in the eyes of God than another. Know that you are truly brothers and sisters and that he or she who loves and supports his little brothers and sisters who may need his help on the Earth plane, is truly light-filled. And so we say to you today what has been said in many ways throughout all time ~ go and love one another and allow the vibrations of your love to fill your souls, your bodies and your world.

Food

Food, essentially, is fuel for the physical body, and as such, it comes in all shapes, sizes and colours. Food also comes in many different vibrations, and each vibration has different properties. Certain foods have vibrations of a very dense, or physical, nature. These foods include meat, alcoholic beverages and sugar. Then there are foods which are less dense, and these foods include grains, vegetables and dairy products. There are foods which have a high vibration, and these are foods which are conducive to spiritual pursuits. These include: fruit, nuts, juices, seeds and berries. We would suggest that you eat what makes you feel good. If you do eat food of a higher vibration, you will come to enjoy an increase in rate of vibration overall. You will come to enjoy a feeling of lightness within your physical body, as well as an opening to an expanded consciousness. We would suggest that if you choose to release the low vibration of red meat, poultry or fish are good to fall back on. These foods have vibrations that will not slow one down in a physical sense. They offer a good source of protein. If you wanted to eliminate these, too, from the menu, there are excellent non-flesh substitutes from which to choose. We would suggest that you eat your food with full consciousness and pleasure. In this way, it will be smoothly assimilated into fuel for physical expression. We would suggest that you give some thought to what you incorporate into your self.

> Know that each kingdom on Earth was created to support your lives here in a multitude of ways. Know that the mineral, plant, animal and devic kingdoms each possess all that you need to both heal and enlighten yourselves. All knowledge and all power, as you know it, is contained within these kingdoms. You have the ability to tap into each one of these in order to receive information and healing. You have the ability to incorporate the wisdom of each kingdom into yourself and grow, as a result. The time has come to planet Earth for all kingdoms to join together in conscious communication and sing the same song of love.

The Food Chain

At the top of the food chain, we find plants and vegetables that take their energy from the sun and rain. This also includes their offspring such as fruits, nuts and seeds. In terms of vibration, these are the very highest that you can take into your physical body. Next, there are products made from this group. These include bread, pasta and so on. Next come dairy products such as milk, eggs and cheese. After this, come poultry and fish. This is followed by red meat in all its forms.

When one eats food from the top of the food chain, one takes in high vibrations that provide the purest energy, or fuel, into the physical body. This results in a feeling of lightness within the physical, as well as mental and spiritual self. The body simply runs better on this fuel. This does not mean to say that everyone needs to do this, but those who do will receive certain benefits from doing so. As this planet passes from the third dimension into the fourth, one of the transitions will include a shift of consciousness in regard to food. This shift will result in many people evolving into a vegetarian lifestyle and we would suggest that this is progress.

Vegetarianism

In the future, vegetarianism will be the diet of planet Earth and it will come about as a reflection of an expanded consciousness. Vegetarianism involves a commitment on several levels. It involves a commitment on the level of spirit. This means that when one undertakes vegetarianism, one chooses to honour the free will, goals and integrity of the spiritual beings that animate the bodies of animals. Vegetarianism also involves a commitment on the level of mind. This commitment is a mental one that acknowledges that the abstention of flesh from a diet is synonymous with an increase in the rate of vibration, and an improvement in overall health. Vegetarianism is also a physical commitment in which one consciously selects and prepares food that provides alternatives to flesh. The commitment here involves a re-education of eating philosophy and practice. Indeed, we would suggest that when one commits to the principles of vegetarianism, one needs to learn new things about food, and how the human body incorporates it into itself.

Know that we do not say embrace vegetarianism. We say only that this is a consciousness which is becoming increasingly more prevalent. We say eat with consciousness and enthusiasm. We say enjoy your food, give thanks for it and enjoy the abundance that is yours.

Dear hearts, when you live in integrity, when you come from a place of authenticity and you do your best to be who you are, and not who you are taught to be, you live within the state called grace. From the state of grace, you are able to access that which you want to experience in the world and this is because the energy of integrity is like a key in the door of All That Is. It opens the door of possibilities that would otherwise remain locked. From the state of grace, you find yourself going with the flow and the flow takes you to where you want to go. Be who you are, dear hearts, for who you are is wondrous.

The New Age

The new age is a shift of consciousness that takes place as we move from third dimension density to fourth dimension. This is happening now as the Earth makes her transition, and all life upon her makes an equal transition in consciousness and ascension. There have been many speculations as to the actual process of ascension. Let us say this ~ that the process will affect each individual according to his or her state of consciousness at the time. For many people, the shift will bring about an end to their physical existence for this lifetime. For others, the shift will bring about the dawning of a new consciousness. And for others, the shift will accelerate their present consciousness into God consciousness. The shift, from the third dimension into the forth, is a process that is underway now and the results, when it is completed, will be truly wonderful. The light that will radiate from Mother Earth will be dazzling. Know that this is both a process of evolution and ascension. We would also like to say that as the time draws closer to this magnificent event, there will be an increase in communication between all species, as well as other life forms. In other words, consciousness will be expanding and borders will be dissolving. This is a prominent feature of the new age.

Lightbody

As you make your way through life, you will encounter energies that are very much in alignment with your own. That is to say, that you will gravitate toward beings with whom you are in increasing resonance. Know that as you do so, you will accelerate the vibration that you are ~ you will begin to speed up the essence of who you are. You will begin to vibrate at the speed of light, and when this occurs, you will transform yourself into what is called your lightbody. As a result, you will access your true intergalactic self: this will bring you freedom beyond your wildest dreams, and this will bring you home.

Know that you who read these
words, are blessed and loved
beyond anything you can
imagine, by your Creator.

Love

Love, as we have said before, is the highest vibration of all and it is the vibration that will bring mankind to God-consciousness. When we, in angelic form, look at a person who is filled with this love, we see a radiating white light that stretches out past the aura itself. This light is wonderful to see. When an individual is able to hold this vibration within them, they are perfectly aligned with God, and this, in turn, aligns them with the God in them. With this perfect alignment comes total health, and total love for all of creation.

If a person, through free will, chooses to grow in this direction, they will receive much help from our kingdom. We would help them from their dream state, as well as from a conscious level. Remember to ask for what you want, and you will receive it. What is asked for in light, will be given in light. We would also suggest that an alignment with the totality of light, love and consciousness is the aim of each soul, and when it achieves this, it may return to its source. The soul is ever on its journey home and when it comes into an alignment with God, then all places are home to it.

Light

Light itself, no matter what its form, all has the same source. Light is the visible vibration of love; it is as bright as its vibration.

When light emanates from living beings, we call this an aura. The aura is a visible representation of the being's energy field. It gives information on the state of the individual's physical, mental, emotional and spiritual health. It gives a read-out of the soul's vibration, so to speak. The light of the soul itself, however, will often extend out past the aura itself. The higher the vibration that the individual has, the brighter this white light shines. We, in angelic form, are able to see this light, and it is wonderful to behold. We are also able to see the lights of all souls shining at once and this is also wonderful. The time is coming to planet Earth when the light that emanates from the souls of all life will truly illuminate the cosmos. This is the time of God consciousness, when heaven manifests on Earth. This is the time of Light.

Forgiveness

Forgiveness brings healing to hearts. It is not well understood in this dimension, but in other dimensions, forgiveness plays a large role. Along the path of light, the human heart becomes bruised and sore. The mind will attempt to address these hurts, but the mind is often limited in its ability to effect change ~ the mind is unable to release pain. It is the heart that does this, and the method that it uses, is forgiveness. When you forgive, you literally let go of the pain. The pain blocks energy that could otherwise be used for growth. We would suggest that you begin to clear the pain from your heart by choosing to forgive whatever or whomever you feel brought it in. The procedure is simple. When you have a clear picture, feel your heart open, and send a ray of light from it to the picture in your mind. As the light surrounds the picture, say, either aloud or to yourself, "I forgive you." This need not take long. Know that as you do so, your heart is being healed. We suggest that you do this with each of the hurts that you have been holding on to. Know that you can heal them all in this manner. Know that forgiveness heals both the receiver and the sender simultaneously, and that forgiveness truly is divine.

Happiness

Happiness is the natural state of the soul and the soul is in alignment with itself when it is happy. There is much within life to lure the soul from its natural state of grace, or happiness. There is much within the day-to-day experience that can decrease the naturally abundant supply of happiness. We would suggest that happiness become cultivated in much the same way as faith and hope. That is to say, that we suggest becoming conscious of one's supply and taking steps to protect it and replenish it when needed.

It need not be difficult to be happy in this dimension, although on the face of it, there is much to both drain and impede it. If you can become aware of what it is that makes your soul feel light, then this is the direction to follow. When you do what it is that fills you with happiness, then all else follows.

The universe is designed to support you in doing what makes you

> *The grand purpose of life is to be happy ~ it is what we are all here for. The more you do what makes you happy, the more you help the world. For the world needs happiness and joy and the way this vibration will enter more fully into this dimension, is by people expressing it.*

happy. As we have said on several occasions, life was never intended to be a struggle, and if more people began to do what fills them with joy, it would benefit all. We would also like to say that we, in angelic form, work with you to bring the vibration of joy into your consciousness. We do this in any way that we can. We work to bring the soul into its natural state of alignment with happiness.

Do what makes you happy. Do what makes your heart sing.

Know that there is an unlimited resource from which you are able to draw at any time ~ this consists of beings who are not residing in the third dimension. You may ask for information of any kind, and receive it. You may ask for healing of any kind, and receive it. You see, the Universe is designed to support you on all levels of your life. Everything that you can imagine is in place to enrich your life experience. Indeed, there is more help available to you than you can imagine. From our perspective, you need only formulate your desire and then ask for the assistance that you require. Do you need technical answers? Consult those who are experts in the field, who are in spirit, and benefit from their experience. Do you need inspiration for the novel that you are working on? Ask an author here to guide you in it's development.

Dear hearts ~ ask and you will receive.

Hope

Hope is the emotion that we, in angelic form, work with most often. It is the vibration of hope that we bring to the hearts of people, for hope is a precious commodity that runs out quickly. It becomes lost in any number of ways in the course of day-to-day living. It becomes lost slowly and one often does not know that it has been siphoned out. The way that we bring hope back into hearts is this ~ we bring the vibration of hope from our dimension, where it abounds, into yours. We do this at all levels of your consciousness. In your waking consciousness, we put things into your path that will re-kindle hope. For example, we will bring an inspirational book to your attention, or we may set up a meeting for you with someone who is brimming with hope and enthusiasm. Or we may prompt you to experience something in the media that triggers these feelings. On an unconscious level, we will work with you in a similar way. The effects of work on this level are often more profound, because people have no resistance to growth on this level.

We would also like to say that hope, although it is easily lost, is also relatively easy to protect. We suggest that people become conscious of their supply of hope, and when they feel it run low, begin to nourish it.

We would suggest surrounding oneself with positive, life-supporting energy and avoiding people, places and situations that do not nurture hope. We, in angelic form, are always working to fill your heart with light, love and hope. We are always working to keep you in touch with your own light, and your own source of hope.

Know that you are a child of God; therefore you are light-filled and strong. Do not believe in failure. Do not believe in lack. Believe in God and light and love, and let your spirit rise up out of your day-to-day consciousness. Let your spirit go free and then follow it where it leads. We are right here, cheering you on.

Meditation

Meditation is the way that the soul connects with its source. In meditation one is able to tap into every dimension of existence and connect with every aspect of oneself. In other words, with every other portion of itself that is experiencing physical expression. At any one time, a soul has many selves that are living at the same time, and in meditation, one can join with them. From a meditative state, simply intend to do so. This experience is a positive one because it gives an opportunity to the soul to feel unity in itself. From a meditative state one can also transcend time and space to learn even more about the nature of life. Again, all one needs to do, is desire to have this experience. From a meditative state one can also tap into the records of the history of this planet, which are often called the Akashic records. In these records are contained every event that has happened here, no matter how little or big. The benefit of doing this is a fresh perspective on the day-to-day experience of consciousness. We suggest that meditation is a tool for connection and empowerment; we hesitate to use this word because it is used frequently, nonetheless, it is the correct word. We recommend meditation as a way of both grounding and expanding.

Prayer

Prayer is the link between God and man ~ it is the way that man communicates his soul's desires. Every prayer that goes out on a vibration of heart is duly heard and answered. The prayer that is not sent out on the vibration of heart does not reach its destination ~ it does not get answered. If people only knew what a powerful tool prayer is, they would use it more often. It is a way of connecting with God and making things happen.

Do not forget to ask for what you need ~ it will be given to you in joy.

There is no limit to what one may ask for in prayer, nor is there a right way to do it. The heart makes its own rules and will find its own way. The only thing one need do is to put the prayer out with one's heart, and then release it. We will take the prayer to God and God will answer it. When a person prays, he or she is making a spiritual phone call, and the call is always answered. We suggest using prayer to put into motion the wheels that connect you with all of life. That is to say, that prayer puts you in a position where you are able to manifest for yourself what you need by sending out a strong signal to the source of all energy. We encourage you to ask for what you need. It will be given to you.

Know that, as you ascend with Mother Earth and move into other vibrations and dimensions, you will feel as if you are living within an answered prayer. You will enjoy that which you can scarcely conceive of at this time. You will experience a level of freedom that eludes you now, and you will remember why it is that you wanted to be here. Your soul will dance in exhilaration with All That Is and your joy will know no bounds.

Peace on Earth

Peace on Earth is more than an idea, it is actually here. Now this does not sound true, or accurate, nonetheless, it is. Peace on Earth lies in the hearts of those on this plane who love peace. Those people, despite the precarious conditions of the world around them, really do experience peace on Earth ~ therefore it is attainable. When more and more people choose peace, whether consciously or unconsciously, the world will reflect it. The world is increasingly ready now to experience peace on a global scale. As it does, it will re-align itself with its own agenda. Yes, even planets have agendas. When peace becomes a way of life on planet Earth, it will once again become a beautifully shining jewel within the cosmos, for peace is composed of a high vibration that emits much light. It is second only in brightness to the vibration of love. The world will grow brighter as people upon it light the candle of peace within their hearts, and nurture the flame.

Ascended Masters

Throughout time and space, there have been entities that have come to the Earth plane in order to emit and spread light to mankind. These masters have appeared in all parts of the globe, and have assimilated into the culture in which they have lived and taught. Ascended masters are entities who have attained God consciousness, and who have chosen to return to the physical plane once more in order to help raise the vibrations of all with whom they come in contact. They are generally not interested so much in gaining followers as they are in disseminating spiritual truths. Some of the most well known masters are: Jesus the Christ, Buddha, Mahatma Gandhi, and Lord Krishna. There are, of course, many more. These masters are committed to light and love and the totality of consciousness. They are committed to being a living example of what humanity can be. Each individual has the potential to realize his or her full spiritual blueprint and ascended masters serve as reminders of this.

Freedom

Freedom is a concept that appeals to mankind because mankind seldom feels free. We would suggest that there is nothing but freedom. Mankind is as free as it wants to be. People have free will in which to create the circumstances of their lives. People have the freedom to choose the beliefs that will create the reality that they experience. Moreover, they have the freedom to change anything in this reality at any time. When one decides to exercise one's freedom to create a new experience, one becomes sovereign over one's own life. If a person feels unfree, let him look to his, or her beliefs (which he or she has freely chosen) to see where they have led him, or her. For when you look to your beliefs, you begin to see where you have allowed yourself to give up your freedom, little by little. Even a person in prison has freedom to choose how he or she will act, think or feel. We

> *Know that all paths have heart. All paths lead home. And as you move along your path, you will be helped by God himself, and God will wear many faces.*

would suggest that freedom is all around and that freedom is the governing principle within the universe. It is more than a concept or an idea; it is ever present and ever available.

Know that you create your world through your beliefs. Choose to believe in absolute freedom, both for yourself, and for others. Choose happiness, dear heart. Choose happiness and freedom and light.

Know that you can achieve, and live in, a state of happiness by choosing your thoughts, rather than by allowing thoughts to choose you. This is the way that it is done: focus upon the thoughts that uplift you. Focus upon the thoughts that inspire you and upon what makes you smile and laugh. Focus upon that which delights you and sustains you. By choosing such thoughts, and putting energy into them, your heart will be happy. From this state of happiness, from this vibration, all good things flow effortlessly into your experience.

Free Will

Free will is the operative law on planet Earth. Free will is important because it is what allows man to make conscious choices that affect the entire fabric of his life conditions. In other words, free will is what makes man sovereign unto himself. Without free will, man would be unable to determine the course of events that form his existence. He would be unable to create growth. He would be unable to move into light. He would be unable to go forward into the direction of his heart, or spirit. Free will is a gift from God that releases man from the wheel of fortune and sets him free.

Know that you have the entire kingdom of God within you and that therefore you can go anywhere, and do anything. You have wings that are strong enough to carry you past all limitations and you are able to rise above all which would hold you down.

Art

Art is something that facilitates a state of transcendence. When one has experienced art, one has experienced an increased rate of vibration. Art is a conduit for transcendental experience. It is not restricted to what is traditionally defined as such ~ it is any aspect of life that is raised to its highest expression. Everyday living can be transformed into art. Every action can be brought up to an art form.

When one performs the simplest action with full consciousness and attention, this is called Zen. We would suggest that Zen is the action component of art. When the action produces a product, as well as the experience itself, this product is called art. Indeed, they are two sides of the same coin. When one transforms one's life into an art form, and turns each action into a conscious experience, one is actually honouring the God that exists both inside and outside of everything.

Are you enjoying your adventure here? You CAN.

Music

Music is powerful because of its ability to transcend time and space. Music on Earth is a reflection of music on the higher planes. True music carries the vibration of light in such a way that it raises the vibrations of those who hear it. This is what art does ~ it allows a transformation to take place within the individual who participates in it. Art raises consciousness by raising vibrations.

Music has different components to it. It is composed of harmonics, scales and numbers. It is also composed of human emotion which gives energy and life to the sound. The time is coming when music will be used for healing the human body, as it has been used in the past to heal the human heart. The way this will be done is by using specifically designed music to raise the frequency of the body to the frequency of perfect health. This will come soon in Earth time. Music that is channeled from the fourth, fifth, or even sixth dimension will be used.

Religion

Religion is man's attempt to organize spirit ~ something, we suggest, that is inherently un-organizeable. It is like trying to organize the weather, so to speak. Religion is man's attempt to understand God. As God's emissaries, we would suggest that the way to understand God is through the heart, not the mind. God is the Big Picture, and we would suggest that the way to perceive it is through the eyes of the soul. It is on the soul level that you are able to understand spiritual truths.

Religion is, as we have mentioned, rather limited in its approach to God. We are not saying eliminate organized religion, we are saying know that religion is merely an idea about God. We are saying that God is larger than any container that man may put him in, in order to study him. We would say that if you long to know God, begin with yourself, for you are God. You are God, and so is all of life. Learn to see God everywhere you look. Notice what God looks like. Notice that God is enormous in his multiple expressions. See how God is the very air that you breathe. See how God cannot be limited by words, thoughts or expression. God is limitlessness. God is more than philosophy and more than dogma. God is all and all is God.

Thought

Thought is what makes things. Everything began as a thought. Now because thoughts are powerful, they can direct energy in a tangible way. Positive thoughts create positive energy and negative thoughts create negative energy. The intensity of the emotion behind the thought determines the speed at which the thought manifests as form.

When a person thinks the same thoughts over a sustained length of time, these thoughts become a pattern. This pattern of thoughts becomes a belief, and this belief will, by and large, remain unquestioned. Positive beliefs do not pose a problem here. Negative beliefs, however, do, because they perpetuate a negative reality. This negative reality is unfortunate and unnecessary. We would suggest that you examine your beliefs to determine the causes of ongoing problems in your day-to-day life. The experiences that you have are determined by your thoughts and beliefs. We would suggest that once a belief has been brought to consciousness, it can then be changed. When a belief has been altered,

Let your intuition guide you in all things ~ it will take you in the best direction.

so will the manifestations of it. This is the law of free will in action ~ free will allows for change and progress. We would also like to say that if you change your thoughts, you are changing your consciousness. When you change your consciousness, you change the world. When you change the world, you bring light into where it is needed.

Know that the sun that you see in your sky is more than what meets the eye. The sun functions not only as a light source, but also as a transmitter of Source energy. In this way, being outside in the sun becomes a healing experience. If you were to expose yourself to the sun with this in mind, and ask for healing from Source, you would receive it. You would receive healing on a deep cellular level. Dear hearts ~ let the sun shine upon you.

Kindness

There is an old saying which goes as follows: 'when in doubt, do the kind thing'. We could not say it better! Kindness is what the world needs more of, and is what the prevailing vibration of the new age will be. Kindness has within it elements of love and empathy. If you were to 'do unto others as you would have them do unto you', you would always do the kind thing. We would also like to say that we feel it would be a good idea to not only do the kind thing, but to think the kind thing, for when we think kind thoughts, kindness returns to us. Know that the vibration of kindness is what you would liken to a jewel within a crown. In all the world, there is nothing so precious to God as a kind heart.

Know that wisdom is related to the heart and not to the mind.

Gratitude

Gratitude is a conscious acknowledgement of one's blessings. When you stop and think of how blessed you are, and then give thanks for these blessings, what you do is put into motion certain laws that then bring more of the blessings into your life. This is what gratitude does ~ it increases what you are thankful for.

If you want to enjoy good health, be grateful for the health that you have now. If you want to enjoy an increase in the money that you have, be grateful for the money that you have now. If you want to enjoy more love in your heart, be grateful for the love that you already have now. If you want to enjoy more peace in your life, be grateful for the peace that you have now.

Be at peace in your day-to-day moments. Be at peace and thank God for the blessings you enjoy.

Know then, that what you put your energy into, increases. Therefore, put energy into that which brings you positive effects. Know that gratitude is the acknowledgement of your blessings, and the more that you focus on these, the more you will receive. We would suggest that there is much indeed to be thankful for.

Humour

Humour is what fans the flame of the soul. Humour is a gift of spirit ~ it has the ability to lift one's soul up from darkness into light. There is an old saying that goes: God respects me when I work, but he loves me when I laugh. How very true this is. The sound of good-hearted laughter is music to the ears of God ~ what a wonderful sound it is. Laughter is the sound track of heaven, if we might be permitted to say so.

Humour is the response to existence that actually makes a lot of sense. In the three dimensional world there is much to look at, and much that, upon examination, is utterly peculiar, particularly within the world of man. The healthiest response is laughter. If one could laugh hard each day, one could do no better in the eyes of God. If one could laugh each day, one would release all pain from the heart, and from the very cells of the body. Laughter truly is the best medicine, and the time is coming when the utter truth of this will be known. The time will come when all disease will not be able to gain a foothold within the human body, because the human body will house a happy heart, and humour and laughter will play a large role in this.

We would also like to say that humour, in all its forms, is present throughout the universe. As a soul ages, so does its capacity to enjoy, share and produce humour. A sense of humour is a lovely gift, and laughter is a sound that transcends all dimensions. It is a sound so precious that it rises up from the Earth plane like the sound of tinkling bells, and fills our hearts.

Dear hearts ~ know that there truly is nothing new under the sun. The universal laws that governed this, and all planets in ancient times, are the same laws which are in effect today. Therefore, that which individuals have accomplished in the past, which you identify as miraculous, can be done again. A miracle is simply an action which is created through intention and brought into form with a conscious knowledge of natural laws.

Children

In children lie the hopes of mankind. In children lie the aspirations of evolution and ascension. In each generation, children represent a surge forward in consciousness. Children, particularly when they are young, are very close to their source, which is God. As a result, they are very pure in their being. They are actually straddling two dimensions simultaneously for a number of years. This generally changes about the age of seven or eight, when they begin to focus on the third dimension. At this time, children begin to relegate their fourth dimensional experiences to the realm of imagination. Generally speaking, it is society that dictates that the world of imagination is not a 'real' world. We would suggest, however, that the world of imagination is very real indeed. Moreover, the faculty of imagination is a powerful and creative arena.

Children are bringers of light from the fourth dimension, where they have been before entering into physical expression. They therefore carry in with them a quality of wisdom that shines from within them, and this wisdom brings its own counterpart of joy. This does not mean that every child is a happy child; it just means that each is very close to the source from which these vibrations originate. We would entreat those with youngsters to honour the powerful life force that they are. We would suggest that raising children is a privilege first and foremost, because children are the light of the world. We would also like to say that children express the ability for giving unconditional love and adults often learn this from children. Unconditional love is what God shows to us all, and unconditional love is the direction in which we are all moving.

Know that all of the great teachers who have come to your planet to work have been happy souls. They all shine with the energy of love. We use the present tense because whether they are using physical bodies or not, rest assured that they are still available to you. Know this and avail yourselves of their vibration. But know, too, dear hearts, that some of the greatest teachers on your plane use the bodies of animals to do their work. Many are what you would call masters. They teach unconditional love and the love that they transmit, heals. Know that even the animals whom you call wild, are your teachers. They teach and hold the space for healing on the spiritual level. Dear hearts ~ thank you for honouring the teachers.

The Soul

The soul is the part of a being that represents the essence of them. It is the part of you that remains the same, lifetime after lifetime and it encompasses the experiences gained throughout all its earthly and off-earth expressions. The soul is a flame that never goes out ~ it is the centre point of life. In the past, a common belief has been that only human beings possessed souls. The truth is that all sentient beings do. Animals have souls. Indeed, to the extent that all life has consciousness, all life has souls. The nature of souls may differ from life-form to life-form, but all life reflects God and all life contains experience. When an entity leaves the Earth plane temporarily, or permanently, the soul is what continues on ~ it remains intact and does not change form. If the soul has chosen to not take another physical form, it then joins with the light from which it comes and then enjoys ultimate freedom of consciousness without physical limitations.

You can choose to make your life an expression of love with everything that you do, think and say.

The word soul is used interchangeably with the word heart, and this is correct, for the heart and soul are the lights of the world. When we, in angelic form, look at the Earth plane, the light we see streaming from it is light that is emanating from souls. The higher the rate of vibration, the brighter the light. The soul's flame grows brighter as it grows in experience and old souls can become bright indeed.

We would suggest that you begin to open to the energies that are all around you; to the light that is available to you. Ground yourself in the Earth and centre yourself in the vibration of love. We would also suggest that you begin to want to experience the joy of your soul. You do this by saying: "I open to receive the joy of who I am." For your soul, dear heart, is who you are.

The God of You

Who you are is God. As God, do not worry ~ worry is for those who do not realize their own identity. As God, do not be afraid of anything whatsoever. Love with all your heart ~ love everything and everyone no matter what level of light they are expressing on. Love without reservation or judgment. As God, smile a lot. As God, be as generous as you can, as often as you can. Give everything you have, as God gives to you. As God, be aware of as much as you can: begin to see what God sees. And finally, as God, be who you are completely. Be all the colours and shapes and dimensions that you are. Be alive. Be very alive. As it is written, when you become the God of you, everything else is added to your experience of life that you require.

*Do not worry about your life.
Spend each day as it comes and let
tomorrow take care of itself. It will.*

Faith

Faith is always difficult to both establish, and maintain, in the third dimension. The reason for this is that in this dimension, people are trained to have faith in what they can experience with their senses. To believe in what they cannot perceive, is certainly a challenge. Nonetheless, some of the finest things there are, are wholly invisible. We would suggest that you have faith in even more things that are invisible and yet are extremely powerful, and present. We would suggest that you have faith in the God within you, and the God within all life. This is not an easy thing to do in the third dimension, and yet we would suggest that doing so would help the transition into the fourth dimension. We would also suggest that you have faith in the continuity of consciousness. We would like you to have faith in our kingdom, as we have in yours. The time is coming, of course, when you will no longer need faith, because you will see us for yourself. You will come to understand all things, and you will find that your faith in the unseen world has been justified. We would also like to say that the day is coming to planet Earth when all of life will have faith in itself, and its relation to God.

Dear hearts ~ know that on the broadest level, everything is perfect. This is much easier for us to see from the dimension in which we reside, than from the one in which you are focussed, but nonetheless, it is true. Everything that you have chosen to create is unfolding according to your desires. Remember that you are often not fully aware of your desires. When you become aware of them, you come to see what a powerful creator you are. When you come to see what a powerful creator you are, then you begin to desire that which aligns you with the God of you. The more that you do this, from the conscious level, the more that you come to see and experience the perfection of All That Is.

Know that we, in angelic form,
are ever with you and
there is a world of spirit
that walks with you
along your journey into light.

LaVergne, TN USA
02 June 2010
184619LV00003B/1/P